olympic
MOSCOW

TEXT: **GUEORGUI DROZDOV**
PHOTOGRAPHS: **NICOLAI RAJMANOV**

1st. Edition, March 1979
I.S.B.N.
84-7424-087-5

CRESCENT BOOKS
New York

There is nothing more pleasant to an ambassador than to introduce the city to which he has been assigned, where the 1980 Olympic games will be held. When this occurs in a capital like Moscow, a city which encompasses such a varied, complex significance, this feeling takes on a special meaning.

The most important elements that can comprise a large city are found in the Soviet capital. Set in the center of Old Russia, Moscow presides over the northern industrial pole as well as the southern agricultural area. These two regions are inhabited by 36 million people, all of whom are gifted with a truly unique working capacity.

If to these two facets —industrial and agricultural— we add the facts that Moscow is the political capital of the huge Federal Republic of the U.S.S.R., the artistic center of an old country, and a city of beautiful monuments, functional architecture and modern avenues, we have easily described the profile of one of the most interesting cities in the world.

The harmonious equilibrium of Red Square, the pale tones of the Kremlin, the inspired architecture of St. Basil's Church, the clasicism of the Bolshoi, and the intensity of its musical life, add unique touches to this magnificent city.

If one feared anything missing to complete this description of Moscow, it would be an elaboration of its student life. The schools and universities in Moscow, along with the number of students, place the city among the first cities in the world in this respect. As a consequence of a well-planned educational system, one witness an increasing quality in competitive sports. When the International Olympic Commitee granted Moscow the organization to host the XXII Olympic games, it was a just acknowledgment of its high rank in the sports arena. Moscow's athletes figure among the best in the world. Its swimmers hold world records. Its gymnasts dominate tournaments and competitions. Its teams always strive for first position. And the competitive attitude of the Soviet people is always an example of respect towards the opponent, of relentless struggle, spectacular effort, and the highest competitive standards.

As the host of the coming 1980 Olympic games, Moscow has completed its sport facilities. The graceful line of its central stadium in Lenin Park, its chain of arenas and sports complexes, the Olympic course for rowing competitions, the secondary stadiums, the gymnasiums and training tracts, make Moscow one of the three olympically best equipped cities in the world.

If a visit to Moscow is a gift in itself for tourists, scientists, industrialists, or art lovers, for the sportsmen it is a real-life adventure.

J. A. Samaranch
Ambassador of Spain in the U.S.S.R.
Chief of Protocol of the International Olympic
Committee.

Moscow, the historical and beautiful capital of the Soviet Union, is one of the largest cities in the world. It covers 878,8 square kilometers, and according to the census of January 7, 1977, it is the home of 7,819,000 people. Another million people, mainly businessmen and tourists, visit the city everyday, coming from all parts of the U.S.S.R. and other countries. The highway that circumscribes the city is 109 km long.

The heart of a huge country that stands out not only historically but in all fields of commerce, industry, art, science, and culture as well, Moscow is today one of the world's vital centers.

The city has a radial and circular structure that developed throughout its history, and in its center, on the hill by the banks of the Moskva River, stands the Kremlin (fortress). As early as in 1147 — usually considered as the founding year of Moscow— a group of people lived in the site where they had built an earthen wall surrounded by a wooden stockade; the place now occupied by the Kremlin.

A lot of water has since then flowed down the Moskva River, faithful and constant eyewitness of everyday life in the city. Moscow suffered the invasion of the Batu Khan hordes, the raids of the Golden Horde of the Crimean Tatars, the Polish intervention in 1612, the unsuccessful attack by Napoleon's troops in 1812, the bloody skirmishes of the first Russian Revolution of 1905 in Krasnaya Presnaya and the entry of the victorious detachments of revolutionaries into the Kremlin in 1917. In December 1941, the German Army suffered a decisive defeat near Moscow; this was the first sign of the fragility in Hitler's plans and of the future Allied victory in the 2nd World War.

Moscow had to withstand severe trials over more than 8 centuries of history. The small city began early in the 12th century, around the Principality of Vladimir-Súzdal. At the beginning of the 15th century the city became the Great Principality of Moscow, uniting most of the Russian territories. In the 16th century during the reign of Ivan IV, known as Ivan the Terrible, Moscow was already, as mentioned by the English traveler R. Chensler, larger than London and vicinities. Moscow remained the capital of the Russian State until the middle of the 18th century. Even after Peter I proclaimed St. Petersburg as the capital, Moscow kept its position as the second capital of the empire and remained as one of the most important Russian industrial centers. Following the October Revolution, the Soviet government was moved back to Moscow in March, 1918, establishing it as the capital of the new Socialist State.

In recent years, the city has been modernized and beautified according to an appropriate plan; house-building was increased, the layout of the streets was improved, new public parks and gardens were established, the renowned subway system was built...

Once again, in 1980, Moscow will become the center of the world's attention, as the site of the Olympic games. Hundreds of thousands of athletes, media people, and visitors will arrive in our capital for this great event. The people in charge of the organization of the games have made a great effort to assure that the Moscow Olympic games pass into history together with the name of this old and beautiful city whose heart beats with the same strength as that of the young people that will visit it.

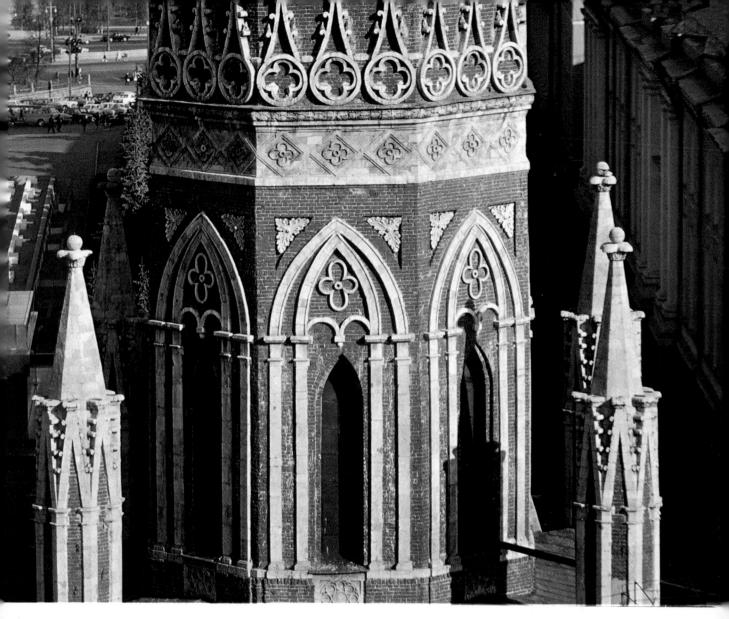

Red Square, formerly called "the Beautiful," is the center of life in Moscow as well as the historic core of the capital. The square, surrounded by the red walls of the Kremlin, has become the symbol of Moscow.

Dostoevsky, the great chronicler of the Russian soul, has left us his account of those Sunday walks that the took as a child with his parents around this square.

At the left were the tall façades of those commercial houses where the large, famous and very rich Moscow shops used to be; to the right, the bright and multicolored St. Basil's Cathedral, one of the most beautiful buildings in the city. This structure combines the variegated mixture of styles so commonly seen in Slavic Art. A perturbing legend tells how Ivan the Terrible blinded the architect who constructed the cathedral to prevent him from constructing another similar work elsewhere in Russia. Red Square in today still the life center of Moscow as well as the sentimental heart of all the Soviet Union. On holidays solemn ceremonies take place here, as well as public demonstrations and large parades. We find here the tomb of the founder of the Communist Party and of the Soviet Union, V. I. Lenin (upper photograph). Behind the tomb, along the wall of the Kremlin, we find the cemetery where the bodies of the fighters of the Revolution and other heroes of the Soviet Union lie. In the photograph on the left we can see the tombs of the following revolutionaries: S.M. Budionny, K.Ie. Voroshilov, A.A. Zhdànov, M.V. Frunze, M.I. Kalinin, F.E. Dzerhinski, Ia.M. Sverdlov, I.V. Stalin, and the remains of the first cosmonaut, Iuri Gagarin.

On the following double page we see a panoramic view of the Kremlin: on the lower left, the Palace of Congresses (1961), where the great assemblies of the Party take place, as well as conventions of Soviet Institutions, international congresses and forums. The Hall of the Palace, fully equipped, has a seating capacity of 6,000 spectators. The Palace of Congresses also functions as a secondary stage for the famous Bolshoi Theater. At the right, the Arsenal Building and the trophies of 1812, seized from Napoleon's troops.

In the building of the Council of Ministers of the U.S.S.R. one finds the commemorative museum "Office and apartments of V.I. Lenin at the Kremlin." From 1918 to 1923, after the Soviet government was moved to Moscow, the founder of the Communist Party lived here.
In the photographs: Monument to Lenin at the Great Garden of the Kremlin; the rooms of the residence, and his working table.

In the upper photograph, a panoramic view of Red Square and the Kremlin: to the left, in the foreground, the building of the Museum of History (1878-1933); in the middle, the Arsenal Tower (1941), the Grave of the Unknown Soldier, and the Arsenal Building (1736). In the lower photograph, the avenue of the embankment of the Kremlin.

From right to left; The Middle Tower of The Arsenal (1495), the gates of the Troitskaya Tower of the Kremlin (1494), and the Grave of the Unknown Soldier.

Above: The old Manezh Building (1817), used today as the Central Exhibition Hall, is found at 50th Anniversary of the October Revolution Square; the Troitskaya Tower, the Kutafia Tower (16th century), and the bridge. In the photographs below: the Nikolskaya Tower (1491) and the Museum of History; the colonnade of the Manezh Building, the Kutafia and Troitskaya Towers of the Kremlin, as seen from the Bell Tower of Ivan the Great (1505-1580); the south wall, and the Great Kremlin Palace (1838-1849)

In the upper photographs: A view of the western landscape as seen from the Troitskaya Tower, the Komendatskaya, Oruzheinaya, Borovitskaya (1940), and Vodovzvodnaya (15th century) Towers at the Kremlin.

A view to the east as seen from the Troitskaya Tower: the Middle Tower of the Arsenal, and the Arsenal Tower; in the distance, the Moskva Hotel.
In the lower photographs: the south wall of the Kremlin with the Beklemishevskaya (1847), Petrovskaya (1819), Blagoveschenskaya (1487-1488), and Vodovzvodnaya Towers; in the distance one can see the Great Stone Bridge (1938).

In the following double page: The main tower of the Kremlin, the Spasskaya Tower (built in 1491; its upper part, including the carillon was built in 1625). The carillon in existance today, whose bell strokes are daily broadcast at the beginning and signing off of Moscow Radio, was installed between 1851 and 1852.
In the other photographs: the bells of the carillon, the dial and the clock hands, and a detail of the ornamentation of the tower.

In Red Square, next to the Spasskaya Tower, we find the masterpiece of Russian architecture, the world renowned Pokrovsky Cathedral (St. Basil's Temple, 1555-1561). In front of the cathedral, the monument to the national heroes Kuzmá Minin and Dimitri Pozharsky, erected in 1818; these heroic men led the popular resistance in 1612 and liberated Moscow from the foreign invaders.

The highest point in Moscow in the 1930s was the Bell Tower of Ivan the Great, 265 ft. high. This tower is the original central point in the architectonical arrangement of temples at Kremlin Cathedral Square. In the photographs, Kremlin Cathedral Square, and in the middle, the Bell Tower of Ivan the Great.

Tourists browsing at the Kremlin.
The world's largest bell, the Tsar Bell, cast in 1735; it weighs 200 tons and
is 20,5 ft. high. The Tsar Cannon was cast in 1586; in its heyday it was
the piece of artillery with the largest caliber (890 mm.). The cannon was
part of the defense of the Kremlin.

An inscription on the top floor of the Bell Tower of Ivan the Great proves that the temple was finished in 1600.

In the photographs at the right: The Terem Palace. The lower stories of the palace have been conserved since the 15th and 16th centuries, the upper levels were built between the years 1635 and 1636. Interior of the Throne Room at the Terem Palace. On the left, the railing of the Golden Chamber of the Tsarina, and a detail of the ornamentation of the Palace.

On the following double page a detail of the facade of the Faceted Palace (1487-1491), one of the oldest public monuments in Moscow. Its name comes from the facing of engraved faceted white stone. To the right, the golden domes of the Verjospassky (early 16th century), and Uspensky (1475-1479) Cathedrals, under the setting sun in winter; interior of the Faceted Palace.

The cathedrals of the Kremlin. From left to right: Blagoveschensky (Annuntiation), 1484-1489; Uspensky (Assumption), 1475-1479; and Arjanguelsky (Archangel Michael), 1505-1508; mausoleum of the Muscovite Tsars and Princes.
In the following two photographs we can see a 12th century mural painting at the Arjanguelsky (Archangel Michael) Cathedral; the tombs of Ivan the Terrible and his sons; and the sculpted portrait of the Tsar made in accordance with his skull.

On this page: the domes of the Blagoveschensky Cathedral (Annuntiation); the interior of the Uspensky Cathedral (Assumption); the iconostasis of the Rizpolozhenie Church (1486), and the golden doors of the Blagoveschensky Cathedral (Annuntiation).

In the following double page we can see unique masterpieces of easel painting, kept at the Uspensky Cathedral: "The Virgin of Vladimir," of the Byzantine school, (late 11th century-early 12th century); and the icon of "St. George" of the Novgorod school (12th century).

Interiors and halls of the Great Kremlin Palace; this construction
is comprised of buildings of different styles, such as the Faceted
Palace, the Tsarina's Golden Chamber and the new wing of the
Palace (1838-1849) or St. George Room; diplomatic receptions,
awards ceremonies, and other official acts take place in this room.
Further ahead we find the interior of the former "Tsar's
appartments," now belonging to the museum. On the right, the
Vladimir Room.

The Armory Halls. The museum was created early in the 19th century, with the treasures of the great Muscovite Tsars and Princes. The objects on exhibition are closely related to the history of the Russian State, and when admiring them, we are reminded of the distant Russian past.
Interior of one of the halls at the museum. To the right, the Tsar's robe.

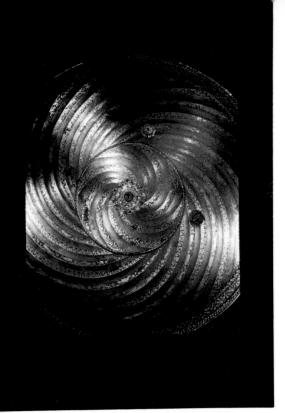

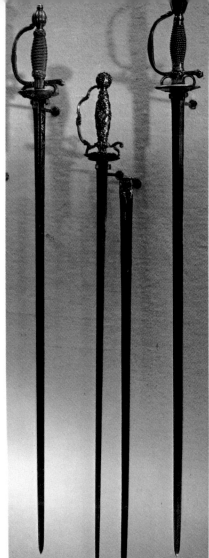

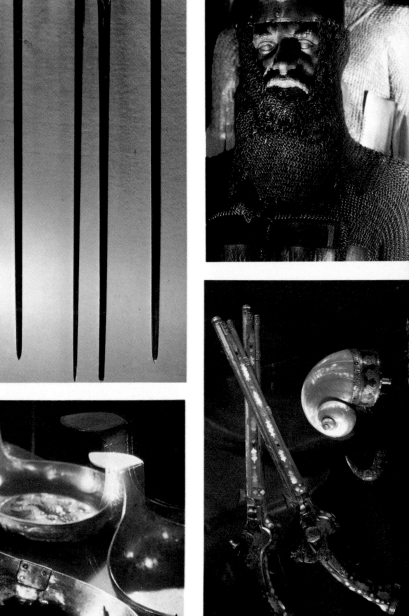

In the photographs: a shield, swords, golden ladles, protective armor for Russian soldiers, pistols, and a gunpowder pouch

The Armory is renowned for its superb collection of varied ornamented pieces and jewels as well as its collection of diverse old weapons, including west European suits of armor. Here one also finds the world's largest collection of carriages from different centuries.

At last, the famous "Cap of Monomakh," used to crown the Russian tsars between the 15th and 17th centuries. This masterpiece of Oriental art (13th-14th centuries) is related to the legendary power inherited by the great Russian princes from the Byzantine emperors.

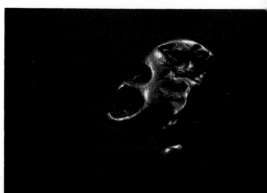

*In the Kremlin Armory in Moscow there is a permanent
exhibition of the U.S.S.R. Diamond Reserves. Here there are
unique precious stones and jewels on exhibition, dating from the
13th to the 19th centuries, as well as the world's largest
diamonds, gold nuggets, and silver and gold jewelry by Russian
and Soviet smiths.*

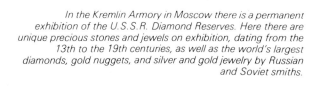

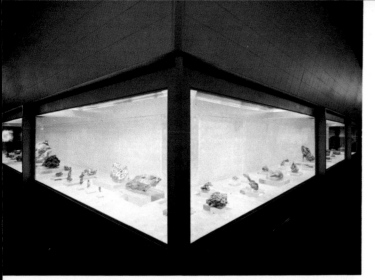

A showcase with jewels: the crowning attire of Russian Emperors,
an emerald brooch, and the order of the "Golden Fleece."

Before leaving the Kremlin and beginning our visit to other points of interest in Moscow, let us have one more look at its adjoining neighborhoods from the high towers.

In the photograph to the left, the building of the U.S.S.R. Council of Ministers; behind it stands the previously seen Museum of History, the State Departament Store (late 19th century), the Moskva and Metropol Hotels, the Bolshoi and Maly Theaters, and several other buildings.

In the upper photograph, the beginning of Gorki Street, one of the main streets of the city. To the left, in the foreground, the National Hotel (1903), and in the background, the new skyscraper of the Inturist Hotel (1969). In the photograph at the bottom we can see a crowd leaving the Kremlin by way of the Kutafia Tower.

This double page includes photographs of the streets and the embankment near the Kremlin in Moscow: a detail of the Great Stone Fountain over the Moskva River; the Rossiya Hotel, with a capacity for 6,000 guests (1965-1967); the Moskva River by the Kropotkin embankment and the Crimea Bridge (1938); Kalinin Avenue in the vicinities of Arbat Square; in the distance, the skyscraper of the Ukrania Hotel

An interesting tour of Moscow begins at the Kutafia Tower of the Kremlin, passes by Kalinin and Kutuzov Avenues and brings us to the Triumphal Arch, erected in memory of the victory of the Russian troops over Napoleon in the war of 1812.

Everyday scenes on Kalinin Avenue, one of the newest streets in Moscow.

Modern and old architectural styles literally stand side by side to complement and contrast with one another: the old Arbat (lower panoramic view) and the modern Kalinin Avenue.

Moscow protects old architectural monuments. The institutions in charge agreed to create special downtown areas where old monuments are under the State's protection.

To the left, details of the
architectural style in the Moscow
of yesterday. To the right, the
skyscraper of the Ministry of
Foreign Affairs, on Smolenskaya
Sq. (1948-1951).
On the following double page, a
panoramic view of Moscow near
Kalinin Bridge (1957); this
photograph was taken from the
International Commercial Center,
which is under construction at
present and situated on the
Krasnopresnenskaya embankment.
This same view will be enjoyed by
businessmen who will come from all
over the world to attend conventions
when the Center is completed. To
the left of the bridge is Kalinin
Avenue; to the right, the Ukraina
Hotel (1956), and the beginning
of Kutuzov Avenue; in the distance,
the skyscraper on Smolenskaya
Square.

The Triumphal Arch, on Kutuzov Avenue is the final stop of our tour. This arch was built in 1817. Later, during the reconstruction of the city, the arch was dismantled, and in 1968 it was rebuilt next to Poklonnaya mountain. The Military Council of the 1st of September, 1812, was assembled on this mountain under the direction of M.I. Kutuzov (Napoleón's famous opponent), after the Battle of Borodino. Here also Kutuzov decided to abandon the city in order to keep his army intact and achieve the victory. The Triumphal Arch is at present called Victory Arch, in remembrance of the 30th anniversary of the Russian victory in the 2nd World War.

Here we also find the Battle of Borodino Museum, and the monument to M.I. Kutuzov.

Below, on the double page, a few details of the panoramic composition painted by F.A. Rubo (1912) depicting different scenes of the Battle of Borodino.

To the right, a fragment of a bronze ornament from the Borodino Bridge (1912).

Last page: we are again in downtown Moscow, by K. Marx Avenue.
This avenue forms the greatest segment of the semicircular
highway that surrounds the central part of the city from the east,
west, and north sides.
In the upper and left photographs: V.I. Lenin Central Museum; to
the right, monument to K. Marx, erected in 1961; a fountain
at Revolution Sq.; the main hall of the U.S.S.R. Maly
Theater (1824). Below, a view of K. Marx Ave., with
the Metropol Hotel in the foreground (1899-1903),
which has a capacity for 400 guests.

The national pride of Soviet and Russian theatrical arts: the
State Bolshoi Theater that has just celebrated its 200th anniversary.
The tours of the company are always very successful and arouse
great interest worldwide. In the photographs: the colonnade of the
façade of the theater, the stage, and several scenes of the ballet
"Swan lake" and the opera "Boris Godunov."

Walking along K. Marx Avenue, we will soon reach
50th Anniversary of October Square (photograph below). In the
middle, the Moksva Hotel, lodging 2,000 guests (1932-1935);
to the right of the hotel, the V.I. Lenin Central Museum
(1890-1892); farther to the right, the Museum of History that we
have already visited. On the left, the old building of Moscow
University (1786-1793). Above, to the right, the bronze monument
to the founder of the first Russian university (1755), the
great scholar M.V. Lomonosov.
On a hill next to the Kremlin stands one of the nicest public
monuments in Moscow, the V.I. Lenin State Library (this old
building was built in the 18th century, as seen in the upper right
photograph). This is one of the largest libraries in the world
with about 30 million volumes.

Here ends K. Marx Ave. and begins our next tour, which will end
by the new building of Moscow University on the Hills of Lenin.

Among numerous points of interest in Moscow is the State Museum of Fine Arts, bearing the name of A.S. Pushkin. Every year more than 1 million visitors, among them many foreign tourists, come to the museum to admire its masterpieces of art. The museum building (1912); exhibited in one of the museum's rooms: "Portrait of an old woman," by Rembrandt and "The Virgin with the Boy," by Perugino.

We are now at the Novodevichii Monastery, a defensive construction built in the 16th century on the west side of Moscow: General view of the monastery; the bell tower; in the distance we can see the outline of the Moscow University building; a view of the towers and walls of the monastery. There were other similar garrisons around Moscow. In the photograph at the right, another interesting place in Moscow: the Kolomenskoye, once a suburban residence of the tsars. The oldest remaining part of the Kolomenskoye structure is the Voznesenie Church (Assumption), 1532 At present all these monuments are branches of the U.S.S.R. State Historical Museum.

Next to the Novodevichii Monastery, in a curve of the Moskva River we find the Luzhniki sports complex, with an observatory on the highest part on the right bank of the river.
The inauguration of the summer Olympic games of 1980 will take place in the Luzhniki complex. Below, a view of the main arena in the Luzhniki complex, the V.I. Lenin Stadium (1956) with a seating capacity for over 100,000 spectators. In the photographs: A scene from a hockey game at the Sports Palace; the World Hockey Championship will take place here in the spring of 1979. Rowers on the Olympic waterways of Krylatskoie.

Several sport grounds and models where the 1980 Moscow Olympic games will be held.

Before us, a view of the
main pavilion of the
Moscow State University.
This city for the sciences
was built between the
years 1949 and 1953, and
it covers 300 acres. The
main building is 36 stories
high and it stands 700
feet tall; it is surrounded
by several smaller
buildings, 8-9 stories
tall, as seen in the air
view in one of the

photographs on the
following page. The
11-story building of the
School of Letters was
built in 1970; today
other buildings are under
construction.
More than 30,000
undergraduate and
graduate students are
currently studying in the
Moscow State University
from Russia and other
countries.

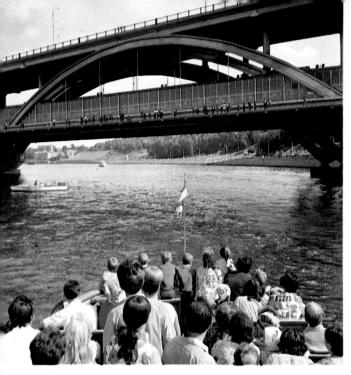

Moscow's subway system is world famous. Its first line was completed in 1935. Today, the subway system has 6 radial lines and a circumscribing one, with construction still going on.

We will only visit a few subway stations: the "Hills of Lenin" station, by the bridge over the Moskva River; entrance to the "Lermontocskaya" station; the underground hall of the "Mayakovskaya" station, and finally, the "Komsomolskaya" station, on the line that goes around the city.

If the Museum of Fine Arts exhibits the best works of western art, the Tretyakov Gallery, south of the Kremlin pass the Moskva River, is famous worldwide for exhibiting the largest collection of Russian and Soviet masterpieces. The gallery bears the name of P. M. Tretyakov, whose collection started the gallery. An outside view of the gallery (late 19th century); icon "The "Trinity" (15th century), by A. Rubliov; a study for the painting "The Zaporozhtsy" (Cossacks of Zaporoznie) "writing a letter to the Turkish Sultan," by I. Ie. Repin; "By the samovar," painted by K. S. Petrov-Vodkin; and a room with old Russian paintings.

On the following double page, the beginning of Gorki Street: the Main Telegraph Building (1930); the Termolova Theater (late 19th century); and the new Inturist Hotel.

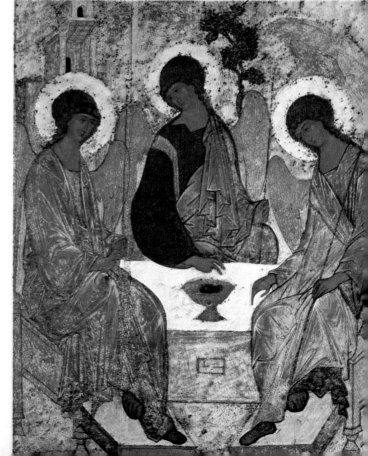

In the photographs we can see: the building of the Moscow City Council of Working Peoples Deputies (1782, reformed in 1945), and the monument to Prince Iuri Dolgoruky, the founder of Moscow. Tchaikovsky Concert Hall (1940) on Mayakovsky Sq., entrance to the Museum of the Revolution (late 18th century); Petrokvsky Palace (1775-1782) on Leningradsky Avenue. To the right, monument to the great Russian poet A.S. Pushkin on the square of the same name.

In the northern part of the city by Peace Avenue, we find one of the attractions of Moscow: The U.S.S.R. Exhibition of Economic Achievements, created late in the 1930s. The Exhibition extends over a surface of 553 acres. Exhibitions dedicated to different economic achievements of the main branches of national economy are constantly taking place in the pavilions. In the photographs: A general view of the Exhibition central grounds; the arcade of the main entrance; exhibition hall at the Moscow International Book Fair in 1977 The Television tower of Ostankino (1967), 1,884 feet tall (twice the Eiffel Tower), near the Exhibition grounds

Right next to The Exhibition of
Economic Achievements stands
the obelisk to the Conquerors of
the Cosmos (1964), 328 feet
tall. This monument was
constructed of titanium, and
erected as a memorial to the
accomplishment of the group of
scientists, astronauts, designers
and workers who planned the
route to the Cosmos.

To the right, ''The
worker and the
Koljosiana,''
monument by the
sculptress
V. Mújina.

The "Cosmos" pavilion at the Exhibition. The objects exhibited are, on one hand, a sample of the attainments by the great scientist and theorist of space flight, K. S. Tsyolkovsky, who, early in this century created the theory of retropropulsive flight of man to the cosmos; and on the other hand, an exhibition of the varied space vehicles, ranging from the first spaceship "Vostok," to the orbital station "Salliut," and the "Soyuz" spaceship. We can also see a few lunar fragments and replicas of the probes that investigated Mars and Venus. In the photographs, several samples on exhibit at the "Cosmos" pavilion; among them, the bronze profile of the world's first astronaut, Iuri Gagarin.

Landscapes in the vicinities of Moscow. House-Museum in Gorkin. Gorki, where V.I. Lenin lived and worked between 1922 and 1924; window of his office and some personal effects on his desk. The museum preserves objects, books, and historic documents dating from Lenin's lifetime.
The town of Gorki is visited by a great number of Russian and foreign tourists, every year.

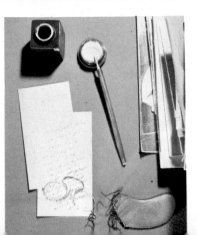

One of the most striking places around Moscow is the *Arkhangelskoye Farm Museum (late 18th century, early 19th century). This was the farm of the well-known architect O. Bove; today it is the National Museum of Architecture, exhibiting masterpieces of Russian genius.*

In the photographs: Different samples of Russian craftsmanship. These objects make fine souvenirs held in high esteem by tourists from all over the world. To the left, the famous Russian "troika" in the meadows around Moscow.

We have come to the end of our short tour of Moscow and its vicinities. We hope that you have received a fine impression of this huge, modern city that keeps its traditions alive and firmly walks towards the future.
We are sure that if you were one of the fortunate visitors to Moscow, this album will be a pleasant reminder of your visit.

If you still have not been to our capital, but will visit it soon whether as a lucky guest at the Olympic games of 1980, or as a tourists visiting the U.S.S.R., we also hope that our album will give you a hand in knowing this extraordinary city better.

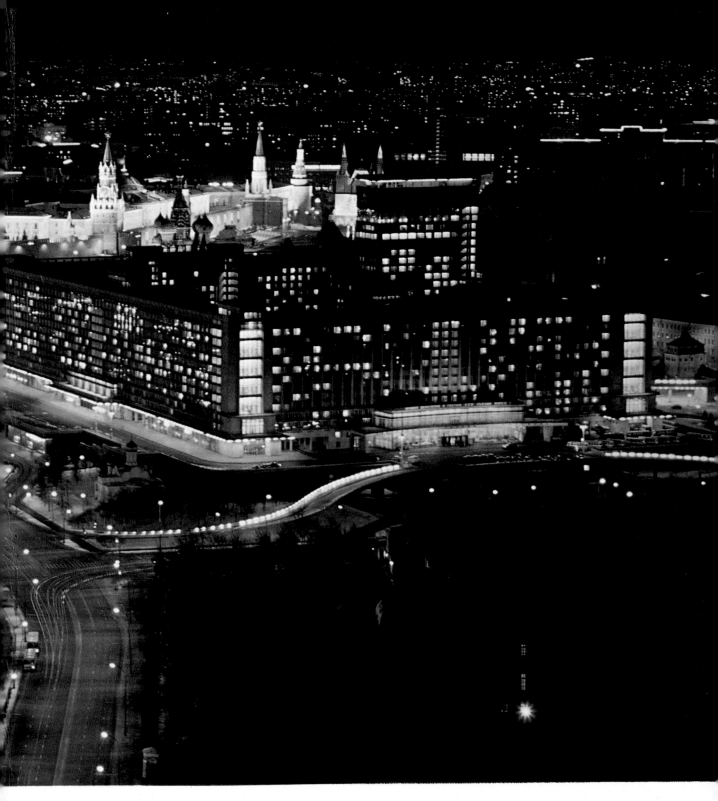

And finally, if you have never been to Moscow, by turning the pages of this album you will mentally cross the barriers of distance, and walk with us along the streets of this warm city, visiting its most attractive sites, and will surely make your intentions of coming here a reality.
Welcome to Moscow!

Printed in Spain  GEOCOLOR®

Travesera de Gracia, 15 - Barcelona (21) - Spain

COGRAF,S.A, Dep, Leg, - B - 16,436 - 79